FORTUNE TELLING

WELBECK
CHILDREN'S BOOKS

First published in the UK in 2025
by Welbeck Children's Books
An imprint of Hachette Children's Group

Copyright © 2025 Hodder & Stoughton Limited

All rights reserved. This book is sold subject to the condition that it may not be reproduced, stored in a retrieval system, or transmitted in any form or by any means, electronic, mechanical, photocopying, recording, or otherwise, without the publisher's prior consent.

A CIP catalogue record for this book is available from the British Library.

ISBN: 9781804539552
Printed in Dongguan, China
10 9 8 7 6 5 4 3 2 1

Welbeck Children's Books
An imprint of Hachette Children's Group
Part of Hodder & Stoughton Limited
Carmelite House, 50 Victoria Embankment
London EC4Y 0DZ

An Hachette UK Company
www.hachette.co.uk
www.hachettechildrens.co.uk

The authorised representative in the EEA is
Hachette Ireland, 8 Castlecourt Centre,
Dublin 15, D15 XTP3,
Ireland (email: info@hbgi.ie)

The publishers would like to thank the following sources for their kind permission to reproduce the pictures in this book.

Shutterstock: Africa Studio 39, 55, 64; Favio Antezana 9, 11, 13; AsilMasterpiece 24; AstroStar 56; Axynia 20; azbotaa 18; Bambooshot 15; beboy 62; Big Blink Creative 49; Blue Titan 28; Samuel Borges Photography 7; Supavadee butradee 37; Cast Of Thousands 22; cloki 35; Cristina Conti 16; Dabarti CGI 66; Dancake 14; delcarmat 45; dezign56 55; dimpank 46; Nejdet Duzen 21; ESB Professional 63; ezphoto 61; Foxartbox 49; fran_kie 16; fukez84 62; Sambhaji Suraj Gaikwad 24; hamid300 19; Hibrida 27; HodagMedia 17; IMG Stock Studio 21; itsmegreat 9; jeabsam 5, 60; dee karen 65; Lina Keil 41; klyaksun 65; Krakenimages.com 10; Andrey_Kuzmin 17; lassedesignen 23; leungchopan 61; LeventeGyori 16; Lost Mountain Studio 9, 50; Maryna Marchenko 52; Marish 46; Alisa Midler 15; MM_photos 35; Mimi Arifa Mohd Jun 67; Dima Moroz 19; mountain beetle 45; Moustachee 59; movit 8; mrjo 20; n_defender 4, 15; Melinda Nagy 45; Navenzeless 23; New Africa 9, 15, 31; Oh_my_stroke 67; ONYXprj 38; oscargutzo 44; Oxanaso 56; Kseniya Parkhimchyk 23; Dasha Petrenko 39; Photoongraphy 55; pics five 9, 34; Anshuman Rath 21; Reytr 54; Prachaya Roekdeethaweesab 5, 17; Roman Samborskyi 12; Sensvector 22; SeventyFour 5; Simply Amazing 48; Sunflowerr 42; valiantsin suprunovich 4, 30, 31; sutadimages 29; Tartila 8, 41; tgergo 25; ThamKC 63; The img 57; thongyhod 49; travelarium.ph 51; TWStock 51; Mark van Dam 55; Yakobchuk Viacheslav 4; viki2win 5, 57; German Vizulis 48; volcano 4, 29; WinWin artlab 19, 42; Wonder-studio 32; xpixel 34; Yellow Cat 63; Mei Zendra 21; COVER LINE ART: **Gettyimages;** Nataliia Prachova; bsd studio; Tatiana Smirnova

FORTUNE TELLING

REVEAL THE MYSTERIES OF THE FUTURE

Contents

Introduction 6

Types of Fortune Telling 8

Palmistry (hands) 10

Scrying (reflective surfaces) 14

Origins of Fortune Telling 18

Oneiromancy (dreams) 20

Numerology (numbers) 24

Is Your Future Fixed? 28

Cartomancy: Tarot Cards 30

Cartomancy: Playing Cards 34

Shaping Your Own Future 38

Astrology: Horoscopes	40
Astrology: The Moon	44
Famous Fortune Tellers	48
Tasseography (tea leaves)	50
Aeromancy (weather)	54
Fact or Fiction?	58
Kau Cim (Chinese fortune sticks)	60
Bibliomancy (books)	64
Quiz	68
Glossary	70
Index	72

Introduction

What does the future hold? Who will I become? Who am I? These are important questions that fortune telling claims to answer. In this book, we look at different methods of fortune telling and how you can shape your own destiny.

Discover how fortune telling and mindfulness go hand in hand.

For centuries, people have turned to fortune-telling practices to learn more about themselves and gain insight into the future. This spiritual practice has attracted its fair share of disbelievers over the years, but it continues to be very popular amongst people of all ages. It is human nature to want to find meaning in things, and that is exactly what fortune telling can offer.

There are many types of fortune-telling methods. Some, such as palmistry (palm reading) and tasseography (tea leaf reading), you may be familiar with, and others, such as numerology (interpreting numbers), may be totally new to you. On the following pages, we look at some of the most popular techniques, as well as tips for how you can improve your life now to achieve the future you desire.

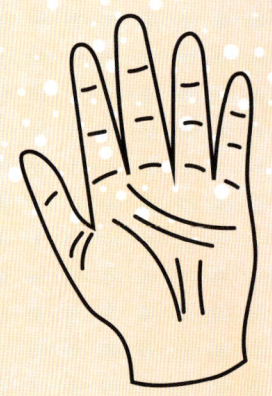

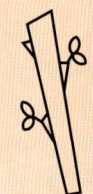

!
ALL IN GOOD FUN

Fortune-telling techniques can offer hope, spiritual exploration and self-reflection, but they should always be taken with a pinch of salt!

Find out about some of the most famous fortune tellers in history and their methods.

THE ESSENTIALS

If you are new to fortune telling, you might feel the need to splurge on tarot cards, crystal balls and fortune sticks. These things can be fun to have, but really, all you need to be a good fortune teller is a quiet space and an open mind!

Get tips on how to shape your own future.

Types of Fortune Telling

There are many methods of fortune telling. Each method has its own unique way of predicting the future, but the basic process is the same: to seek meaning in symbols and situations. How many of these methods do you recognise?

AEROMANCY
(see pp 54–57)

Divination from the weather

ASTROLOGY
(see pp 40–47)

A study of the movements of the Sun, Moon, stars and planets

BIBLIOMANCY
(see pp 64–67)

Divination by books

CAPNOMANCY

The interpretation of smoke patterns

CARTOMANCY
(see pp 30–37)
The art of reading cards

CLEROMANCY
Divination from small, tossed items, such as stones or dice

GEOMANCY
The interpretation of geographic features, such as rock patterns

KAU CIM
(see pp 60–63)
Divination by fortune sticks

NUMEROLOGY
(see pp 24–27)
The study of the significance of numbers

ONAMANCY
Divination by the letters of a name

ONEIROMANCY
(see pp 20–23)
The interpretation of dreams

PALMISTRY
(see pp 10–13)
The art of palm reading

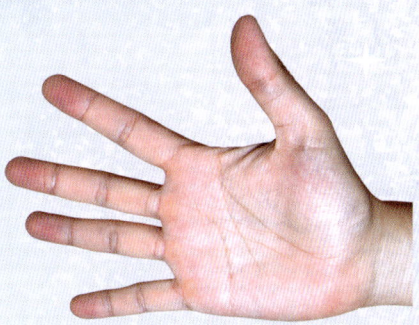

PSYCHOMETRY
Divination by touching objects

SCRYING
(see pp 14–17)
Divination by gazing into a reflective surface

TASSEOGRAPHY
(see pp 50–53)
The interpretation of patterns in tea leaves or coffee grounds

THE MORE YOU KNOW
Divination is essentially another word for fortune telling. It is the practice of predicting the future.

Palmistry

One of the most popular methods of fortune telling, palmistry is the act of palm reading to interpret personality traits and predict future events.

ORIGIN

This practice is thought to date back to ancient India. It spread from there to other parts of the world, including ancient Greece, where it was even used to diagnose health issues!

WHICH HAND?

It's worth studying both hands when palm reading, as they each show different things. The dominant hand (the hand you use most often) is believed to represent the present and future – things like personality and talents – whereas the non-dominant hand is said to reveal potential, such as hidden traits.

BIG BELIEVER

Greek philosopher Aristotle was fascinated by palmistry. His view was that 'lines are not written into the human hand without reason'.

PALM LINES

There are five palm lines in palmistry: head line, heart line, life line, sun line and fate line. From studying these lines, you can learn all sorts about yourself, from how you connect with others to your potential for fame.

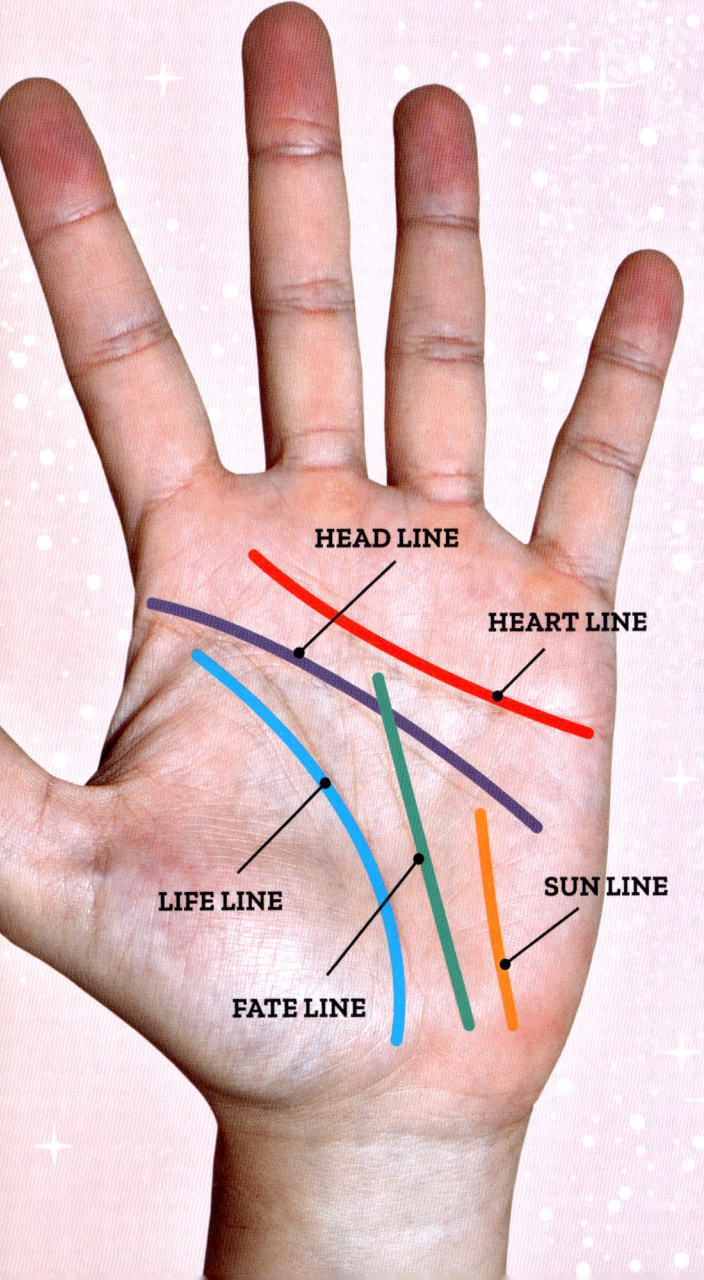

LIFE LINE
FATE LINE
HEAD LINE
HEART LINE
SUN LINE

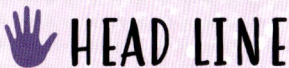 **HEAD LINE**

Reveals: intellectual abilities and communication style

Long / deep head line: analytical, logical
Short / faint head line: creative, difficulty focusing

 **HEART LINE**

Reveals: how you connect with others

Long / deep heart line: passionate, expressive
Short / faint heart line: reserved, guarded

 **LIFE LINE**

Reveals: your energy, health and major life events

Long / deep life line: energetic, resilient
Short / faint life line: low energy, introverted

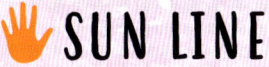 **SUN LINE**

Reveals: potential for fame and success

Long / deep sun line: likely to achieve recognition
Short / faint sun line: personal approach to success

 **FATE LINE**

Reveals: your career path and destiny

Long / deep fate line: strong sense of purpose
Short / faint fate line: spontaneous, open to changes

HAND SHAPES

In palmistry, there are four basic hand shapes that correspond with the four elements: earth, air, fire and water. Each hand shape is associated with different traits. Which type are you?

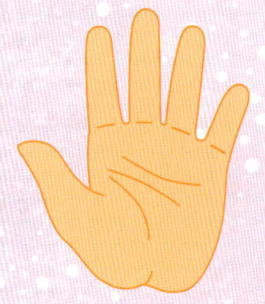

Earth

Square palms and short fingers

Traits: practical, hardworking, dependable

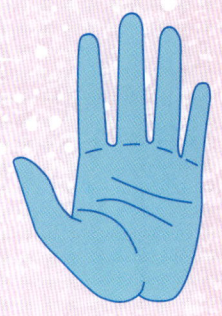

Air

Square palms and long fingers

Traits: active, communicative, curious

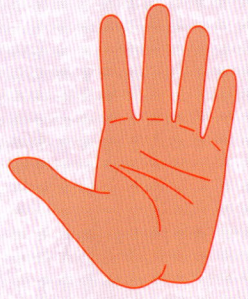

Fire

Long palms and short fingers

Traits: passionate, energetic, creative

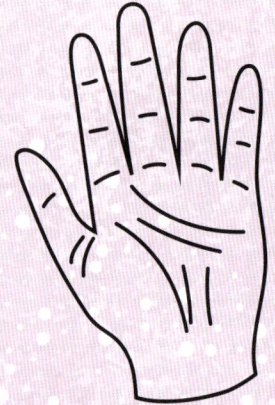

Water

Long palms and long fingers

Traits: caring, sensitive, intuitive

MOUNTS AND PLAINS

The fleshy, raised areas on your palms are called mounts, and the flat areas between them are called plains. Mounts correspond to different planets and represent different aspects of personality. Developed mounts suggest strong traits associated with that planet, while sunken mounts indicate areas for improvement.

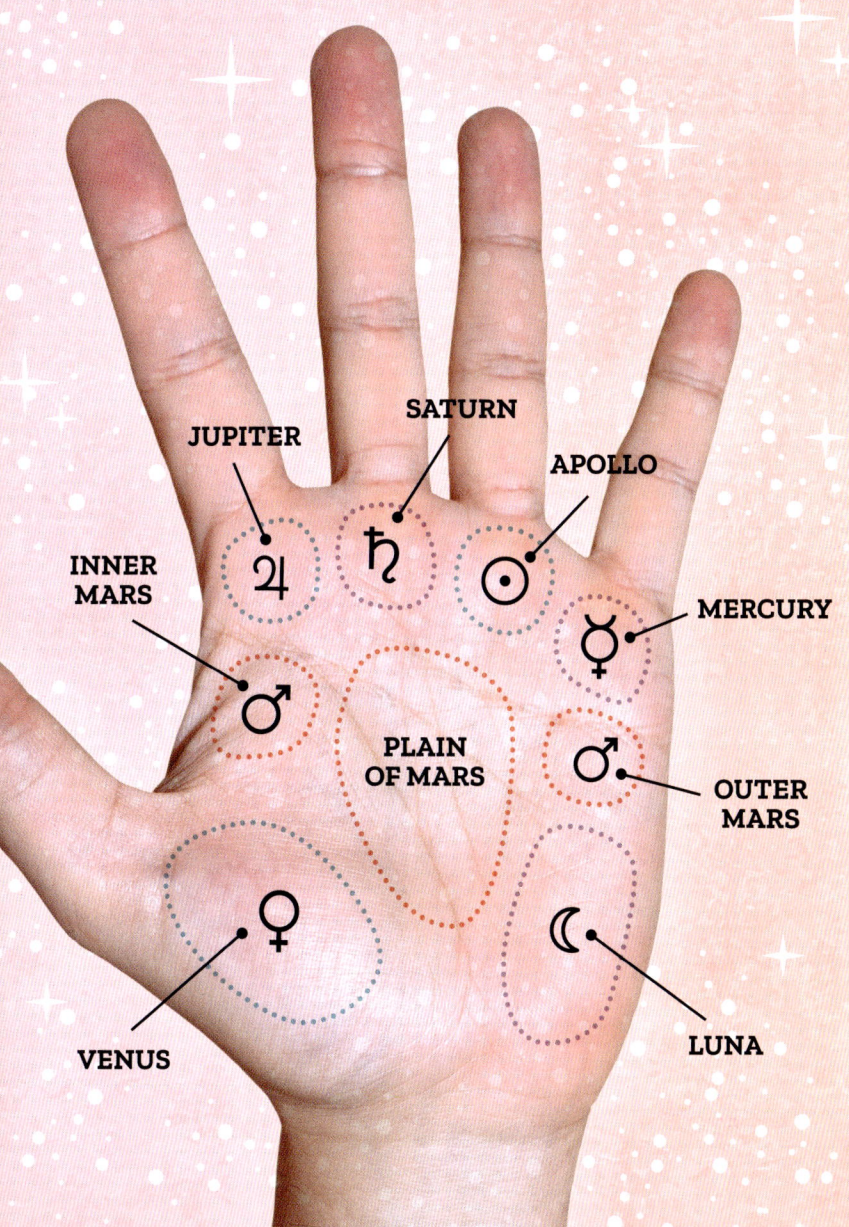

♃ JUPITER
Symbolises confidence, ambition and power

♄ SATURN
Relates to wisdom, discipline and introspection

☉ APOLLO
Linked to optimism, vitality and creativity

☿ MERCURY
Connected to communication, wit and intelligence

☽ LUNA
Symbolises imagination, intuition and compassion

♀ VENUS
Linked to love, affection and charm

♂ MARS
Inner Mars: Related to courage, adventure and physical strength
Outer Mars: Represents self-control, bravery and perseverance

Scrying

This famous method involves gazing into a reflective surface to receive insights into the future.

ALL-SEEING

The word 'scry' comes from the Old English word 'descry', which means 'to see'.

ORIGIN

Scrying can be traced back to China in 3000 BCE. It was also used in ancient Egypt and ancient Greece, before gaining popularity in medieval Europe.

HOW IT WORKS

Scrying requires a reflective medium, such as a mirror or bowl of water, and a clear head. Scryers are encouraged to empty their mind through meditation, as this is thought to make them more open to messages. Once in a peaceful state, they are ready to gaze upon their medium and wait for visions to appear.

TYPES OF SCRYING

There are many types of scrying. Here are some of the most popular . . .

CRYSTAL SCRYING

When you think of fortune telling, you likely think of a crystal ball. A crystal ball is actually a common scrying tool. Its reflective surface provides a soft focus, allowing the scryer's mind to wander and visualise images.

MIRROR SCRYING

Mirrors work in a similar way to crystal balls. They are another type of reflective surface that scryers can use to receive messages. They also have the added benefit of being readily available!

WATER SCRYING

Also known as hydromancy, water scrying involves looking for symbols in water. This could be a bowl or cup of water, or a much larger reflective surface, such as a pond or lake. This method was made popular by French seer Nostradamus.

WHO CAN DO IT?

Fortune tellers are often portrayed as Romani women with crystal balls. In reality, many cultures practice scrying and it is not limited to any gender!

CONNECTION TO THE SUBCONSCIOUS

Scrying is a way to tap into the subconscious mind. The subconscious is the part of your mind that you are not aware of. It is believed to contain all of your memories and to influence your behaviour. The symbols that appear in a scrying session can reveal a scryer's secret hopes, dreams or fears.

COMMON CHALLENGES

Some challenges with scrying include getting in the 'zone', being unable to see images, being unable to interpret images and differentiating between flights of fancy and true insights. With patience and practice, a scryer can overcome these difficulties and have fun scrying.

FAMOUS PREDICTIONS

Nostradamus, one of the most famous seers in history, was a fan of scrying. His method involved gazing into a bowl of water or a mirror to fall into a trance and see the future. His book, Les Prophéties (The Prophecies), records his predictions*, which are said to include...

- The French Revolution
- The rise of Adolf Hitler
- The Challenger Disaster
- The Great Fire of London

Nostradamus

A prediction by Nostradamus that is believed to be about the Great Fire of London in 1666. Some think the 'ancient Lady' refers to London itself.

The blood of the just will be lacking in London,
Burnt up in the fire of '66:
The ancient Lady will topple from her high place,
Many of the same sect will be killed.

*It's worth noting that Nostradamus wrote his prophecies as poems, and they are open to multiple interpretations! Several versions also exist.

The Origins of Fortune Telling

Fortune telling has its roots in ancient China, Egypt and Babylonia. Evidence suggests it was practiced as long ago as 4000 BCE!

CHINA

Two of the earliest methods of fortune telling in China involved using tortoise shells and yarrow stalks. In the first method, a tortoise shell was heated and the cracks that formed were interpreted. In the second method, known as I Ching divination, hexagrams were made using yarrow stalks and then interpreted using the *I Ching* text.

I CHING

The *I Ching* is an ancient Chinese divination text that has been used for thousands of years as a tool for guidance. The book is related to the concept of yin and yang – opposing but complementary forces that make up all aspects of life. It consists of 64 hexagrams (a group of six broken or unbroken lines), each representing a unique situation. Used as a method of fortune telling, it can help answer a person's questions.

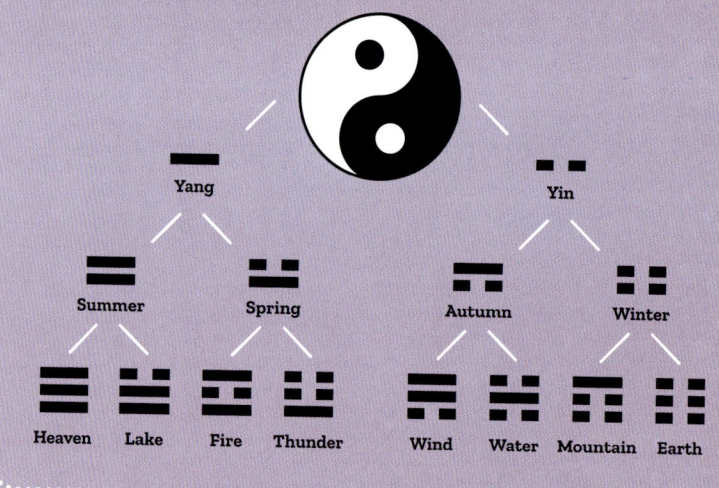

EGYPT

Ancient Egyptians practised oneiromancy (dream interpretation) and scrying to gain insights into the future. Scyphomancy, which is divination using a cup or goblet, is thought to originate from ancient Egypt and Persia.

BEHIND THE NAME

The word 'fortune' comes from 'Fortuna', the Roman goddess of luck.

BABYLONIA

We wouldn't have horoscopes if it weren't for the Babylonians! This ancient civilisation believed the movement of the stars and planets revealed important messages, including the will of the gods. It was a priest's job to interpret these celestial signs.

ANCIENT ROME

The Romans also used divination to discover the will of the gods. Signs included falling objects and the behaviour of birds, and these signs were interpreted by a special priest called an augur.

Oneiromancy

The interpretation of dreams to predict the future is called oneiromancy (oh-NIGH-ruh-man-see). This is slightly different to dream analysis, which generally explores a dreamer's mental state.

ORIGIN

Dream interpretation dates back to ancient Mesopotamia. It was also popular in ancient Greece and ancient Egypt.

MYTHOLOGICAL MESSENGERS

In Greek mythology, the Oneiroi were dark-winged spirits of dreams that delivered messages from the gods.

HISTORY

Oneiromancy is based on the belief that dreams are messages from gods or spirits. It was taken very seriously in ancient times. Ancient peoples regarded it as an art, and it was treated as a science by philosophers and physicians.

PREDICTIVE OR NOT?

Oneirocritica is an influential book on dream interpretation written by Greek diviner Artemidorus in the 2nd century CE. The book emphasises the importance of context in understanding dreams and distinguishes between everyday reflections and predictive dreams. Artemidorus suggests some predictive dreams are literal and others are symbolic.

DREAM TEMPLES

In ancient times, sacred spaces existed for the purpose of dream interpretation. The dream temples of Asclepius in Greece were some of them. Named after the god of healing, they were places people would go to to sleep and hopefully receive healing messages from Asclepius.

FAMOUS PRECOGNITIVE* DREAMS

Joseph's dreams of power
In the Bible, Joseph has two dreams involving his family bowing down to him, foreshadowing his rise to power.

Harriet Tubman's visions of freedom
Abolitionist and social activist Harriet Tubman had vivid dreams that she interpreted as divine guidance, helping her and others to find freedom.

Niels Bohr's Nobel Prize–winning dream
Niels Bohr's dream about the structure of an atom turned out to be correct and led him to win a Nobel Prize.

* This means supernormal knowledge of future events.

WHAT DOES IT MEAN?

It is important to note that there is no evidence to suggest dreams can predict the future. But that doesn't mean that they cannot influence it. Dreams are seen as windows to the soul. They can reveal your hidden fears and desires and encourage you to act in one way or another, shaping your future.

DREAM JOURNALLING

One way to pay better attention to your dreams and what they may be trying to communicate is by keeping a dream journal. In this journal, you can write down the kind of dreams you have, how they made you feel and what they may symbolise. You can then decide if you would like to act on this information.

GOOD DREAMS AND BAD DREAMS

There is no such thing as good dreams and bad dreams in the context of fortune telling. Dreams that appear bad, such as dreams about death or dying, do not foretell future misfortune. Instead, they are more likely to reflect your current mental state, alerting you to issues that may need addressing.

COMMON DREAMS AND THEIR SYMBOLISM

Flying
freedom, empowerment, newfound independence

Falling
anxiety, insecurity, loss of control

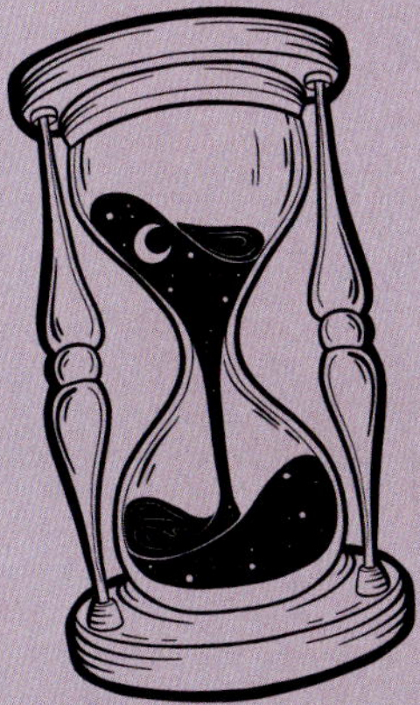

Being late
feeling overwhelmed or unprepared, need for change

Dying
change, rebirth, new beginnings

Numerology

This fortune-telling method is all about numbers. It is based on the idea that numbers have unique vibrational energies that influence our lives.

ORIGIN

Early records of numerology come from the ancient civilisations of Egypt and Babylon. It has roots in mathematics.

PYTHAGORAS

The ancient Greek philosopher Pythagoras is famous for the Pythagorean Theorem (you might've learned about this in maths!), but he is also known as the 'father' of numerology. His followers believed numbers were more than just quantities – they had symbolic meanings that could reveal the secrets of the Universe.

MAKE A WISH

Some people believe repeating 11s are good luck. That is why you'll often hear people say, 'Make a wish!' when it gets to 11:11 on a clock.

THE NUMBERS

The primary numbers in numerology are 1, 2, 3, 4, 5, 6, 7, 8 and 9. You can learn about their significance on pp 26–27. Numerology also has master numbers. These are 11, 22 and 33, and they are extra special because they symbolise a higher vibrational energy. Vibrational energy is associated with emotions. Positive emotions are linked to high vibrations and negative emotions are linked to low vibrations.

LIFE PATH

In numerology, your life path number is said to represent your personality, purpose and potential. It is calculated from your birthdate, but the process is a little tricky, so let's break it down . . .

1. Write down your birthdate

If your birthdate is 1 May, 2015, you would write it as:

1/5/2015

2. Add the digits

Add all the digits together. In our example, it would look like this:

1 + 5 + 2 + 1 + 5 = 14

3. Reduce to a single digit

If the sum is not a master number or single digit, add the digits together until you get a single digit. In our example, we would get:

1 + 4 = 5

4. Once you've got your life path number, turn to pp 26–27 to find out what it means!

NUMBER SYMBOLISM

Let's dive deeper into the symbolism of numbers in numerology. You can also find out what your life path number means and if you can relate to it or not . . .

1 — The **NUMBER 1** symbolises the self. It represents independence, ambition and new beginnings. Those with this life path number are seen as natural leaders.

2 — This even number is associated with balance and harmony. **NUMBER 2** individuals are often described as great peacemakers.

3 — The **NUMBER 3** represents creativity and communication. People with this life path number tend to be enthusiastic and good at expressing themselves.

4 — This number symbolises stability and discipline. **NUMBER 4** individuals are known for their organisational skills and reliability.

5 — The **NUMBER 5** represents adaptability and adventure. If your life path number is 5, you may have a strong desire for freedom.

6 — The 'mother' of the numbers, the **NUMBER 6** represents love in all its forms. These individuals are seen as caring and empathetic.

7 — The **NUMBER 7** symbolises mystery and spirituality. Number 7 individuals tend to be deep thinkers and truth seekers.

8

This number represents authority and balance. Those with the life path **NUMBER 8** are often ambitious, with a strong sense of purpose.

9

The **NUMBER 9** is associated with wisdom and completion. Number 9 individuals are seen as idealistic and compassionate.

MASTER NUMBERS

11 The most intuitive of all the numbers, **NUMBER 11s** are believed to have an old soul and a spiritual connection to the Universe.

22 Known as the 'master builder' number, **NUMBER 22s** are seen as visionary leaders who can turn dreams into realities.

33 A highly influential number, **NUMBER 33s** have the ability to be wonderful, compassionate teachers.

Is Your Future Fixed?

Fortune telling aims to predict future events, implying that the future is predetermined. Many practices, though, acknowledge the potential for change and the importance of free will.

INSIGHT VS PREDICTION

Many fortune-telling methods focus on insight rather than precise predictions. Tarot card reading (pp 30–33) is one of these methods. Tarot can give insight into a person's past, present or future, but it does not claim to predict the future with certainty. Instead, the reader is encouraged to explore potential outcomes.

SAY WHAT?

Some theories suggest that time itself is an illusion – that the past, present and future exist all at once. In that case, you're already in the future!

SCIENCE SAYS...

Fortune telling is not backed by science. It lacks a scientific basis and is not supported by evidence. According to science, the future remains uncertain. However, despite lacking scientific proof, fortune telling continues to be a source of guidance and entertainment for many people.

PSYCHOLOGY SAYS...

Psychology emphasises the importance of mindset in shaping the future. It proposes that thinking positively about the future can motivate a person to make decisions that will lead to desired results, while thinking negatively about the future can lead to anxiety and depression. As your mindset is changeable, this perspective implies that the future isn't fixed.

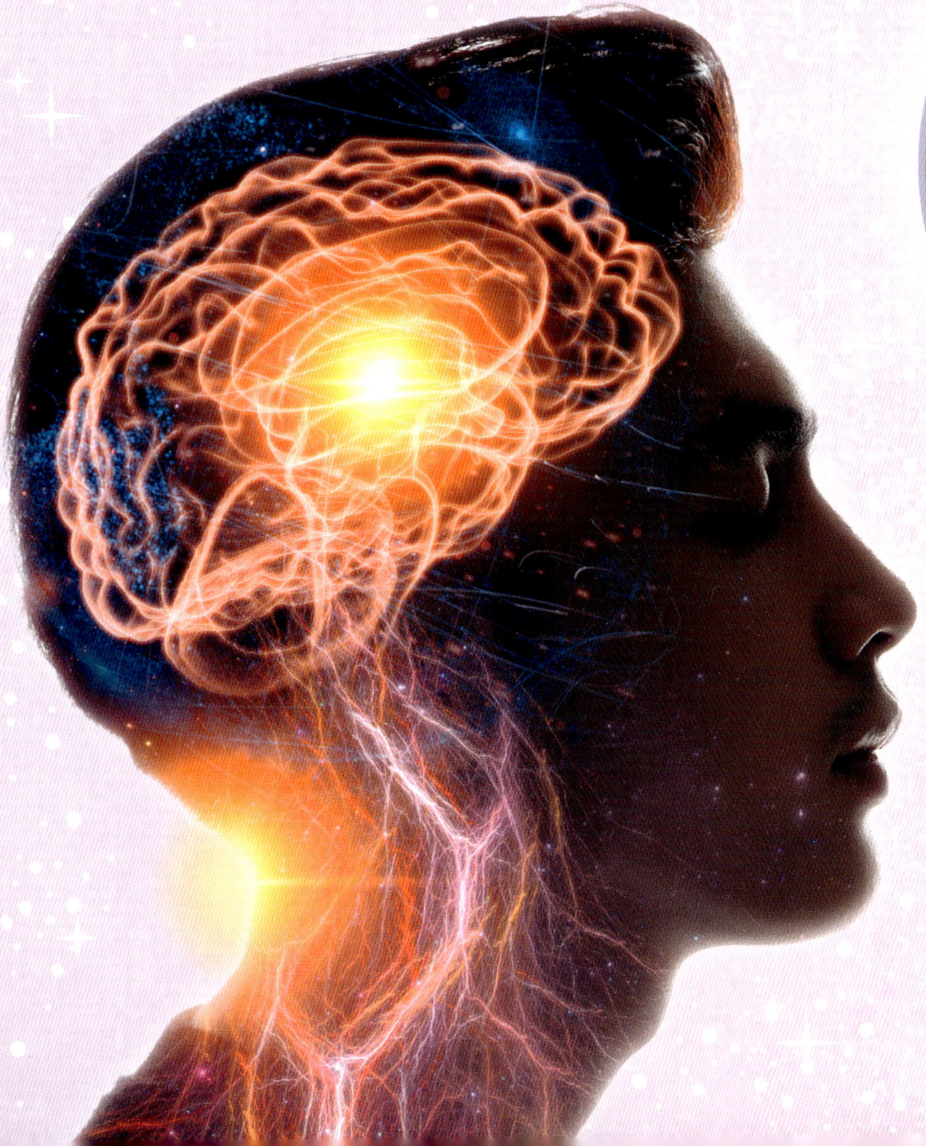

DETERMINISM VS FREE WILL

Determinism and free will are two sides of the same coin. Determinism suggests everything is fixed, while free will suggests humans have the ability to make their own choices and determine their own fates. Whether or not you have control over the future has been a subject of debate for centuries – which side do you fall on?

Cartomancy
TAROT CARDS

Cartomancy is divination using cards. One common form of cartomancy is tarot card reading, which is more popular than ever today.

ORIGIN

Tarot cards date back to 15th-century Italy, where they were used to play a game called tarocchi. They began to be used for fortune telling in France around 1780.

FORGOTTEN ARTIST

The most widely used tarot deck, the Rider-Waite deck, was illustrated by artist, feminist and mystic Pamela Colman Smith, who was almost lost to history.

WHAT IS TAROT?

Tarot is a deck of 78 cards used to gain insight into the past, present and future. Each card has its own imagery and symbolism. Tarot readers ask a question and draw cards at random. They then lay the cards out in a spread, which gives structure to the readings, and interpret the cards in the context of a question.

* The appearance of tarot cards differs between decks.

THE DECK

A standard deck is made of 22 Major Arcana cards and 56 Minor Arcana cards. The Major Arcana cards are the most significant, representing major life events. The Minor Arcana cards represent everyday situations.

BASIC SPREADS

ONE CARD – A single tarot card is a quick and easy way to get an immediate answer to a question.

THREE CARDS – There are many variations of a three-card spread. The most common is the past–present–future spread.

FIVE CARDS – A five-card spread (as seen on the right) may cover themes such as love, family, friendship and general guidance.

EXAMPLE QUESTIONS

What new opportunities await me?

What is the most important step I can take towards my future goals?

What does my future career look like?

What would future me like to tell me?

What do I need to know about ...?

MAJOR ARCANA CARDS

The foundation of the deck, the Major Arcana cards mean serious business! Pulling one of these cards indicates a period of significant change, challenge or growth. Let's take a closer look . . .

MINOR ARCANA CARDS

The Minor Arcana cards are divided into four suits: Wands (action), Cups (emotion), Swords (intellect) and Pentacles (practicality). These cards can reveal the situation you're currently in.

THE HIGH PRIESTESS

This card symbolises intuition, spirituality and wisdom. The High Priestess invites you to trust your gut feeling.

THE SUN

This card signifies joy, success and abundance. It represents a time of happiness and personal growth.

THE FOOL

The Fool represents new beginnings, innocence and a free spirit. It usually appears in readings when you are on the verge of an exciting new adventure.

THE MOON

The Moon represents the unconscious mind and encourages you to explore the hidden aspects of yourself.

THE MAGICIAN
action, skill, manifestation

THE EMPRESS
femininity, creativity, abundance

THE EMPEROR
authority, status, power

THE HIEROPHANT
wisdom, conformity, tradition

THE LOVERS
union, love, harmony

THE CHARIOT
victory, control, determination

STRENGTH
strength, courage, compassion

THE HERMIT
introspection, solitude

WHEEL OF FORTUNE
change, luck, destiny

JUSTICE
fairness, truth, law

THE HANGED MAN
surrender, sacrifice, release

DEATH
transformation, new beginnings

TEMPERANCE
patience, balance, harmony

THE DEVIL
materialism, temptation

THE TOWER
sudden change, upheaval

THE STAR
hope, inspiration, renewal

JUDGEMENT
spiritual awakening, inner calling

THE WORLD
wholeness, completion

Cartomancy
PLAYING CARDS

A standard 52-card deck can also be used for fortune telling in a very similar way to a tarot deck.

ORIGIN

Playing cards are thought to have originated in China as far back as the 9th century. They weren't used for fortune telling until many years later, after they were introduced to Europe in the 14th century.

HOW IT WORKS

Similar to a tarot deck, every card in a standard deck has its own symbolism. Readers ask questions, pull cards and let their intuition guide them. Unlike a tarot deck, there are far fewer cards in a standard deck: 52 compared to 78.

THE FOUR SUITS

There are four suits in a standard deck of playing cards: **hearts**, **spades**, **diamonds** and **clubs**. Each suit represents a different life theme.

HEARTS
emotions, relationships, love

SPADES
thoughts, communication, challenges

DIAMONDS
money, practical matters, possessions

CLUBS
passions, motivation, action

THE EMPRESS'S ORACLE

The most famous cartomancer of all time, Marie Anne Lenormand, advised influential figures during the French Revolution and Napoleonic era, including Empress Joséphine.

SIMILAR SUITS

The four suits in a standard deck correspond to the four suits in a tarot deck like so...

COURT CARDS

The court cards are the King, Queen and Jack.

KING
paternal energy, authority

QUEEN
maternal energy, wisdom

JACK
similar to the Knight and Page in tarot

JOKER
not a court card but a 'wild card' that symbolises new beginnings

NUMBER SYMBOLISM

Each number represents something different in a standard deck, from new beginnings to the end of a cycle.

- **A** — new beginnings, potential
- **2** — balance, relationships
- **3** — growth, creativity
- **4** — stability, structure
- **5** — challenges, instability
- **6** — success, fulfilment
- **7** — wisdom, choices
- **8** — movement, organisation
- **9** — understanding, compassion
- **10** — completion, end of a cycle

EXAMPLE READINGS

Combining all this information on suit and number symbolism, here are some example readings . . .

ACE OF HEARTS
Represents new relationships

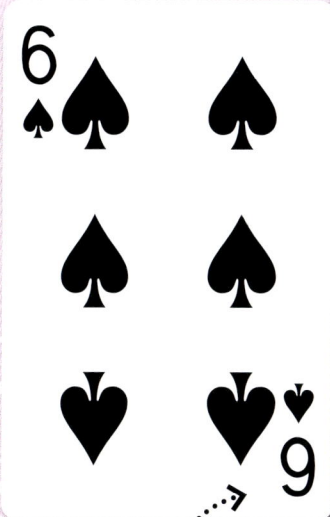

6 OF SPADES
Symbolises small wins

10 OF DIAMONDS
Indicates good fortune

KING OF CLUBS
Represents a period of decision-making

PLAYING CARDS vs TAROT

Playing cards can be a good stepping stone into fortune telling. They are more accessible than tarot cards, and some find them easier to read because of their simplicity. Others may prefer tarot for the visuals, which are magical in themselves!

Shaping Your Own Future

There are many things you can do right now to shape your own future. These things range from setting goals to developing new habits, and their impact shouldn't be underestimated!

USING FORTUNE TELLING

You can enjoy fortune telling and still believe that you have free will. Fortune telling is great for introspection. It can be used as a tool to explore your desires, fears and potential. You can then act on this information to make changes in your life, impacting your future.

GOAL SETTING

What do you want to achieve in the future? Write it down, and then decide what actionable steps you can take now to make that dream more likely. For example, if your dream is to be an Olympic swimmer, you can start by entering local swimming competitions. Small wins eventually turn into big wins!

HEALTHY HABITS

Instead of focusing on the habits you want to have in the future, focus on the habits you have now. These habits shape your future. Some healthy habits include . . .

★ Eating balanced meals
★ Staying hydrated
★ Getting plenty of sleep
★ Being active
★ Practising good hygiene

VISUALISE IT

Sometimes it can help to literally visualise your future. A vision board is perfect for that. It can include images, quotes, affirmations and whatever else may inspire you to achieve your dreams. They're also a lot of fun to make!

POSITIVE AFFIRMATIONS

Your mindset is everything. It is how you perceive the world and your past, present and future. Mindset can be improved through positive affirmations. These are kind words that you tell yourself to boost self-esteem and encourage positive changes, such as 'I am strong and capable' and 'I am in control of my destiny'.

Astrology
HOROSCOPES

Astrology is one of the most popular fortune-telling methods. It claims that the position of the planets and stars at the time of a person's birth can predict personality traits and life events. Horoscopes are based on astrology.

ORIGIN

Astrology and horoscopes date back to ancient Mesopotamia, specifically in the city of Babylon.

WHAT IS A HOROSCOPE?

A horoscope is an astrological chart that represents the positions of the Sun, Moon and planets at the time of an event, such as a person's birth. Horoscopes are used as a tool for self-reflection and guidance, as they are said to reveal a person's personality traits and potential life events.

BREAKING IT DOWN

There is a lot to know about horoscopes. Here are some key concepts and what they mean...

SUN SIGN – Also known as your star sign or zodiac sign, this is the position that the Sun was in when you were born. It is said to reveal your core identity. Find out which of the 12 star signs you are on pages 42–43.

MOON SIGN – This is the position that the Moon was in when you were born. It symbolises the inner you, your emotions and subconscious.

RISING SIGN – Also known as the ascendant sign, this is the zodiac sign that was rising on the eastern horizon when you were born. It represents how others see you.

12 HOUSES – The zodiac is divided into 12 houses, each representing a different area of life. Each house is linked to a zodiac sign. For example, Aries is linked to the house of self, while Gemini is linked to the house of communication.

DEVELOPMENT OF THE HOROSCOPE

The Babylonians developed 12 astrological signs, many of which are still used today. The ancient Greeks later named these 12 signs based on constellations and their alignment with the Sun's orbit. Today, there are entire websites, apps and magazine columns dedicated to horoscopes.

CIRCLE OF ANIMALS

The word 'zodiac' comes from a Greek phrase that translates to 'circle of animals'.

YOUR STAR SIGN

Now it's time to see what your star sign says about you!
Are you fiery like Aries or dreamy like Pisces? Read on to find out . . .

THE ELEMENTS

Star signs are further categorised into the four elements: earth, water, air and fire. Each element represents different qualities.

EARTH
Practicality, patience, stability, reliability

AIR
Intellect, curiosity, communication, adaptability

WATER
Sensitivity, sentimentality, empathy, artistry

FIRE
Passion, energy, enthusiasm, boldness

ARIES
(March 21 – April 19)

Element: Fire
Traits: bold, passionate, impulsive

TAURUS
(April 20 – May 20)

Element: Earth
Traits: grounded, dependable, stubborn

GEMINI
(May 21 – June 20)

Element: Air
Traits: intelligent, playful, indecisive

CANCER
(June 21 – July 22)

Element: Water
Traits: sensitive, caring, creative

LEO
(July 23 – August 22)

Element: Fire
Traits: confident, competitive, loyal

VIRGO
(August 23 – September 22)

Element: Earth
Traits: analytical, hardworking, helpful

LIBRA
(September 23 – October 22)

Element: Air
Traits: diplomatic, persuasive, fair

SCORPIO
(October 23 – November 21)

Element: Water
Traits: intense, determined, independent

SAGITTARIUS
(November 22 – December 21)

Element: Fire
Traits: adventurous, friendly, funny

CAPRICORN
(December 22 – January 19)

Element: Earth
Traits: ambitious, disciplined, honest

AQUARIUS
(January 20 – February 18)

Element: Air
Traits: curious, free-spirited, mysterious

PISCES
(February 19 – March 20)

Element: Water
Traits: compassionate, romantic, imaginative

Astrology

THE MOON

In astrology, the Moon's phases are thought to affect life on Earth, with each phase offering its own strengths and uses.

ORIGIN

Moon astrology, as with astrology in general, has roots in ancient Mesopotamia. Babylonians, in particular, were interested in the Moon's movements and influence.

THE PHASES

The eight Moon phases are: new Moon, waxing crescent, first quarter, waxing gibbous, full Moon, waning gibbous, last quarter and waning crescent. In each phase, the Moon appears differently. For example, it is barely visible during a new Moon but completely visible during a full Moon. This cycle repeats itself once every 29.5 days.

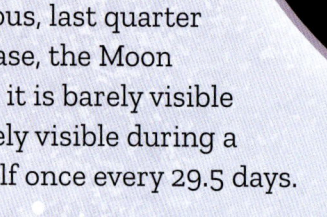

MOON MADNESS

Each phase of the Moon has its own symbolism (more on that on pages 46–47). The full Moon is especially rich in symbolism. Ancient thinkers such as Aristotle and Pliny the Elder associated the full Moon with madness, and the word 'lunacy' even comes from the Latin 'lunaticus' meaning 'moonstruck'. To this day, some people are wary of a full Moon!

OCEAN INFLUENCE

During full and new Moons, the Sun, Earth and Moon align. This creates a stronger gravitational pull on the Earth's oceans, resulting in very high high tides and very low low tides.

MOON WORSHIP

Some ancient cultures considered the Moon to be a deity and worshipped it through unique, celebratory rituals. This celebration stems from the Moon's perceived connection with the rhythms of life and the Universe. In many cultures, the Moon was personified as a goddess, such as Selene (Greek) and Luna (Roman).

MOON CALENDAR

The Babylonian calendar was a lunisolar calendar used in ancient Mesopotamia. It was based on the Moon phases and was mainly used for timekeeping and ritualistic purposes. Each month began with a new Moon, which is linked to new beginnings and was a cause for celebration.

MOON SYMBOLISM

The phase of the Moon when you were born can reveal a lot about you as an individual. It can provide insight into your personality, your strengths and weaknesses, and how you show up in the world. What does your Moon say about you?

NEW MOON

Represents:
- Fresh start
- New beginnings
- Limitless possibilities

Explanation:
Children of the new Moon typically possess a curious, adventurous spirit. They are known to be creative, enthusiastic and optimistic, approaching their many interests with a can-do attitude.

WAXING CRESCENT

Represents:
- Growth
- Intention
- Hope

Explanation:
Those born under a waxing crescent Moon are said to be positive, energetic and ambitious. They tend to face any challenges with enthusiasm, confident in their own abilities.

FIRST QUARTER

Represents:
- Action
- Determination
- Balance

Explanation:
First quarter babies are said to be deeply intense and full of potential. They are seen as changemakers with a mission to inspire others. Their well-roundedness puts them in a good position to do this.

WAXING GIBBOUS

Represents:
- Progress
- Preparation
- Motivation

Explanation:
Waxing gibbous babies are known to be strong and resilient. They can recognise the potential in themselves and others, which makes them excellent, inspiring mentors.

FULL MOON

Represents:
- Celebration
- Gratitude
- Self-reflection

Explanation:
Those born under a full Moon are known to burn fast and bright. They tend to be highly emotional people, driven by passion and a strong desire to be in the spotlight. It can be hard for them to relax!

WANING GIBBOUS

Represents:
- Transition
- Introspection
- Patience

Explanation:
Children of a waning gibbous Moon may naturally be curious about the world around them. They are believed to be intuitive, empathetic individuals, with a strong sense of gratitude.

LAST QUARTER

Represents:
- Reflection
- Understanding
- Release

Explanation:
Children of the last quarter Moon are thought of as sentimental, introspective individuals. They are said to have strong intuition, with the ability to analyse situations with a calm, clear mind.

WANING CRESCENT

Represents:
- Wisdom
- Maturity
- Healing

Explanation:
Those born under a waning crescent Moon are thought to be very wise. They may have a gift for introspection and be drawn to practices like journalling, which allow them to reflect on their experiences.

USING THE PHASES TO YOUR ADVANTAGE

Now you know what each Moon phase represents, you can use the phases to your advantage. For example, the new Moon may be a great time to begin new projects, while the last quarter Moon may be a good time to tie up any loose ends of current projects.

Famous Fortune Tellers

Throughout history there have been many fortune tellers – some more notable than others. From Nostradamus to Marie Anne Lenormand, here are some of the most famous fortune tellers, their methods and their reported visions.

NOSTRADAMUS

1503–1566
French astrologer and seer Nostradamus is famous for his book of prophecies. He used a combination of methods to tell the future, including scrying. See p17 for some of his predictions.

PSYCHIC OR PROPHET?

Psychic, prophet, clairvoyant, seer, soothsayer, mystic and diviner are all terms that can be used to describe fortune tellers.

FORTUNE TELLING ANIMALS?

Some people think animals can tell the future too! Punxsutawney Phil is a groundhog who 'predicts' the weather on Groundhog Day (2 February) every year. And Paul the Octopus gained fame for his successful football match predictions.

BABA VANGA

1911–1996

Baba Vanga was a Bulgarian mystic who had a significant following. She claimed to have started experiencing visions in childhood, after a storm left her blind. Her predictions are said to include the 9/11 attacks and the death of Princess Diana.

EDGAR CAYCE

1877–1945

Nicknamed the 'Sleeping Prophet', Edgar Cayce was an American clairvoyant who claimed to receive visions after entering a trance-like state. He gave readings to celebrities like Harry Houdini and Marilyn Monroe, covering topics such as health and personal matters.

MARIE ANNE LENORMAND

1772–1843

Marie Anne Lenormand was a French cartomancer who famously gave advice to influential figures of her time, such as Empress Joséphine. Her predictions, including Napoleon Bonaparte's divorce from Joséphine (which happened!), often got her into trouble with the law.

Tasseography

This fortune-telling method involves looking for messages found in the patterns of tea leaves. It is also known as tea leaf reading.

ORIGIN

Tea leaf reading dates back to ancient China, the birthplace of tea. It became popular in Europe in the 17th century, when tea was first introduced there.

ITEMS INVOLVED

All that is needed for a tea leaf reading is a cup (a white cup is preferred, so shapes can be seen more clearly), loose leaf tea and hot water. Loose leaf tea is essential because the tea in tea bags is too fine and won't create the best shapes. Any flavour of tea works – as long as it's loose leaf!

THE PROCESS

Tea leaf reading starts with brewing a cup of tea, but with a specific method. The loose-leaf tea is steeped and not strained – that means, the leaves are soaked in hot water. The tea is then drunk, but before it is finished, it is swirled around, helping the leaves to settle and create patterns.

VICTORIAN FASCINATION

Tea leaf reading was popular during the Victorian era, when society was fascinated by the supernatural.

THE SHAPES

A good imagination is needed for tea leaf reading, as the shapes aren't always obvious! Symbols to look out for include animals, objects, letters and numbers. Turn to pp 52–53 to find out the meaning of some common symbols.

THE CUP

In tasseography, the cup is divided into sections. The rim represents the present or the immediate future, the sides symbolise the near future, and the bottom signifies the distant future. The handle of the cup represents the person getting the reading. Shapes that appear near the handle are believed to be relevant to the person's current situation.

PRESENT OR IMMEDIATE FUTURE

PRESENT

NEAR FUTURE

DISTANT FUTURE

COMMON SYMBOLS

The possibilities of what you might come across when tea leaf reading are endless. However, these symbols tend to appear pretty often...

FOLLOW YOUR INTUITION

Tea leaf readings are subjective. This means that they are open to interpretation. Like all fortune-telling methods, tasseography relies heavily on intuition. What do you think you see, and what do you think it means?

A bird in tasseography may symbolise a safe and happy journey or that good news is on the way.

A crescent Moon signifies prosperity and success.

A leaf or leaves indicate change and personal growth. You may be on the cusp of a new journey.

A full Moon symbolises romance.

A heart represents love and relationships. The clearer the heart, the stronger the love.

Seeing a cat in your tea leaves may be a sign to embrace your playful side. It could also be a sign to watch out for deceitful people.

An anchor symbolises stability and security. It is a sign that you feel grounded in life.

Seeing a tree in your tea leaf reading is a positive omen. It suggests that you feel happy in life and are on the right track.

Aeromancy

Fortune telling based on the weather is called aeromancy. A popular type of aeromancy is cloud divination, which involves looking for shapes in clouds.

ORIGIN

This practice has roots in ancient civilisations such as the Greeks and Babylonians. It is thought to have been used by ancient Babylonian priests.

HOW IT WORKS

Cloud divination is very simple. It involves watching the clouds pass by and finding meaning in their shapes. It is one of the most mindful fortune-telling methods, as it doesn't require much effort and promotes relaxation. Simply lie down and observe, letting your intuition guide you.

CLOUD JOURNAL

If you are a creative person, you might like to draw or paint the clouds you see in the sky. This may even help you to interpret their symbolism, as you will be able to keep revisiting them. If writing is more your thing, you could have a special diary for your cloud-spotting observations.

MESSAGE FROM THE GODS

Many ancient cultures believed that weather patterns were messages from the gods. Good weather was interpreted as a blessing, while bad weather was seen as a punishment.

OTHER THINGS TO WATCH FOR

Aside from the shape of the clouds, pay attention to how fast they are moving. Fast clouds may signify your fortune coming quicker. Also take note of how light or dark they are. Fluffy white clouds may symbolise positive emotions, while dark clouds may represent challenges.

MAXIMISING MINDFULNESS

Make your cloud-spotting experience that extra bit more relaxing with these things...

★ A quiet place to lie down and tune out, like a garden or secluded park

★ A blanket and cushions for comfort

★ Sunglasses to protect your eyes

★ Water to stay hydrated – this is especially important if you plan to be outside for a long time

★ A journal to draw or record your thoughts

OTHER TYPES OF AEROMANCY

Other subtypes of aeromancy include wind, thunder, lightning and meteor divination. Like cloud divination, these methods involve interpreting the appearance and movement of the weather phenomena.

THUNDER AND LIGHTNING DIVINATION

With this type of divination, the sound of thunder and the colour and shape of lightning is significant. The date on which thunder occurs is also thought to be important. The Etruscan Brontoscopic Calendar explains what thunder might mean if heard on a certain day of the year. The Etruscans were an ancient civilisation that lived in what is now Italy.

METEOR DIVINATION

This lesser-known form of aeromancy involves interpreting meteors (shooting stars). In many cultures, shooting stars are seen as good luck. Some cultures even believe stars represent souls and that a shooting star represents a soul on a journey. In Greek mythology, shooting stars were seen as signs from the gods.

PRO TIP

If you are interested in practising aeromancy, make sure the weather conditions are safe to do so! You do not have to go outside to observe weather patterns, you can always look through a window in the safety of your home.

WIND DIVINATION

In wind divination, the direction the wind blows is highly symbolic. A south wind is considered good luck, while an east wind suggests change is coming. Wind chimes are a great tool for this type of divination – in some cultures, they are seen to promote positive energy.

Fact or Fiction?

Is fortune telling a form of witchcraft? Was Zoltar a real person? Find the answers to these questions and more here...

FACT

Astrology and astronomy are NOT the same.

Astronomy is the scientific study of celestial objects and the Universe. Astrology studies the movements of planets and stars and how they may influence life on Earth – it is not considered a science.

FACT

Fortune telling can offer short-term comfort.

A positive fortune-telling reading can give a person hope and reassurance. However, it is not recommended that fortune telling should be used to treat mental health problems.

FICTION

Fortune telling is the same as witchcraft.

Witchcraft is the use of magical powers to influence events or even cause harm. Fortune telling is a more casual practice that does not intend to inflict harm. Instead, its purpose is to gain insight into the future.

FICTION

Zoltar was a real person.

The coin-operated fortune teller from the 1980s movie Big is not a real person. He is a fictional character, though you might find him in an arcade or amusement park!

FICTION

All mediums are fortune tellers.

A medium is a person who claims to be able to contact spirits. While some mediums claim to be fortune tellers, they are not all fortune tellers by default. It is also difficult to prove if a person really is a medium or not!

FACT

Zoomancy is a form of divination based on the behaviour of animals.

This lesser-known fortune-telling method has roots in ancient China. It is sometimes referred to as theriomancy, which translates to wild animal divination.

FACT

Fortune telling is still popular today.

Not only is fortune telling still popular today, but it may also be rising in popularity – especially with younger generations. There are hundreds of websites and apps dedicated to exploring the practice, and people continue to consult fortune tellers.

Kau Cim

This ancient Chinese method of fortune telling involves interpreting answers from numbered flat sticks. In the West, Kau Cim is known as 'Chinese fortune sticks'.

ORIGIN

The practice of Kau Cim is thought to date back to the Jin dynasty in ancient China.

THE STICKS

Chinese fortune-telling sticks typically come in sets of 100. These sticks resemble flat incense sticks and are often painted red at one end. Each stick is numbered, and the number on each stick corresponds to a specific fortune. The sticks are stored in a tube, generally made of bamboo.

LOTTERY POETRY

Another name for Kau Cim is 'lottery poetry', which refers to the fortunes often being written as poems.

HOW IT WORKS

Kau Cim begins with an individual asking a question. This question could relate to anything from family to health, and it doesn't have to be said out loud. With a question in mind, the person shakes the container until a single stick falls out. The number on the stick corresponds to a specific written fortune that offers an answer to the question.

EXAMPLE QUESTIONS

★ What is my purpose in life?
★ What path should I take?
★ How can I improve my relationships?
★ What can I expect in the coming months?
★ How can I overcome . . . ?

THE FORTUNES

Depending on the set, the fortunes may be written on separate pieces of paper or they may appear all together in a book. They can be written as poems or more straightforward pieces of advice. Traditionally, these fortunes were interpreted by soothsayers. Nowadays, people tend to use their own intuition or consult the internet!

MINDFUL ASSOCIATIONS

Kau Cim is associated with Taoism, an ancient Chinese philosophy and religion that emphasises living in harmony with the Universe. It is also linked to Buddhism, a spiritual tradition that focuses on personal development and overcoming suffering.

FAMOUS TEMPLE

The practice of Kau Cim is often performed in a Taoist or Buddhist temple in front of an altar. The famous Wong Tai Sin Temple in Hong Kong is dedicated to the deity, Wong Tai Sin, known for his healing powers, and draws in hundreds of thousands of people each year – some bringing offerings such as incense sticks or flowers.

Statues at Wong Tai Sin Temple are touched by worshippers for good luck. This statue is of Yue Lao, the god of love and marriage.

RIGHT OR NOT?

Jiaobei blocks may be tossed to determine if a person's answer is right or not. These blocks are crescent Moon-shaped and made out of wood. They are flat on one side and round on the other. A successful answer requires one flat and one round side to be facing up.

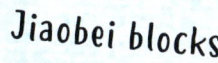

Jiaobei blocks

VARIATIONS

Kau Cim sets vary in appearance and number of sticks. Chi Chi Sticks, which are a US version of Chinese fortune sticks, have 78 sticks. They were introduced to the United States in 1915 by a company based in San Francisco – a city with a historically large Chinese population.

Bibliomancy

The ancient practice of using books to tell the future is called bibliomancy. It is one of the easiest yet lesser-known methods of fortune telling.

ORIGIN

This practice dates back to ancient Roman and Greek civilisations. It has roots in the ancient Roman practice of sortes, which involved interpreting a single line or passage from a book or text.

WHAT BOOK?

All that is needed to perform bibliomancy is a book. Almost any book will do, as long as it speaks to you. The idea is that you think of a question, then, with your eyes closed, you open the book at random, dropping your finger on the page. The words or passage you land on serve as an answer to your question.

POETIC ADVICE

The Sortes Homericae was a type of divination that involved interpreting a random sentence from the works of the ancient Greek poet Homer.

SACRED TEXTS

Bibliomancy is often used with sacred texts such as the Bible. These books are rich in symbolism and can offer spiritual guidance to believers. Non-religious people may prefer using poetry or their favourite novel.

CHOOSING A BOOK CHECKLIST

★ Is the book age-appropriate?
★ Does the book have a special meaning to me?
★ Does it cover the theme(s) I am interested in?
★ Is it easy for me to understand?
★ Is it a mostly happy or sad book? This will influence the kind of fortune you get!

FICTION OR NON-FICTION?

The answer is whichever you prefer! Fiction books can be used for bibliomancy. For example, there is no reason why you couldn't use the *Harry Potter* books for divination – divination is even a subject taught at Hogwarts! However, non-fiction books, such as self-help books or even dictionaries, also work.

ENVIRONMENT MATTERS

It is best to perform bibliomancy in a quiet place, where there are few distractions and you can focus on the words in front of you. A library is great for this, and it's full of books for you to choose from! If one book isn't gelling with you, you can just pick up another. Find a quiet nook and get practising.

INTERPRETING THE WORDS

Finding 'your' words is easy. Interpreting them is the tricky part! If you happen to stumble on a passage that makes no sense to you, before moving on to another book, try asking yourself these questions . . .

★ Are they words of hope or warning?

★ Are they trying to push you towards action or reflection?

★ Is somebody saying the words? Could this person or character be significant?

★ Do the words make more sense in a wider context – for example, when read as part of a paragraph?

★ Was my question specific enough?

EXPERIMENT WITH TECHNIQUES

There are multiple ways to practice bibliomancy. The method outlined on p64 is just the most common. You could also use dice to decide which page or chapter to read from, and instead of picking words from just one page, you could pick one word from multiple pages and combine them to get your meaning. Experiment with it!

WRITING YOUR FUTURE

Some people use bibliomancy for inspiration. For example, some use it as a tool for creative writing. They take the words or passage they landed on and use them as inspiration for a story. Why not do the same? You could even use 'your' words to write a short story about your dream future . . .

Quiz

Let's see how well you were paying attention. Choose the right answer for each of these multiple-choice questions, then see how well you did by checking the answers at the bottom.

Which of these is NOT a major palm line in palmistry?
a. Heart line
b. Sun line
c. Dream line

What is the name of the Roman goddess of luck?
a. Luna
b. Fortuna
c. Venus

What is the name for divination by dreams?
a. Oneiromancy
b. Cleromancy
c. Onamancy

What item is used for cartomancy?
a. Books
b. Cards
c. Chinese fortune sticks

PRO TIP

If in doubt, let your intuition guide you . . .

What does the Moon sign represent in astrology?
a. Your core identity
b. Your emotions and subconscious
c. How others see you

What are the master numbers in numerology?
a. 11, 22, 33
b. 1, 2, 3
c. 3, 6, 9

Which fortune teller was nicknamed the 'Sleeping Prophet'?
a. Nostradamus
b. Baba Vanga
c. Edgar Cayce

What is another name for tea leaf reading?
a. Tasseography
b. Aeromancy
c. Geomancy

Where will you find Wong Tai Sin Temple?
a. Bangkok
b. Tokyo
c. Hong Kong

ANSWERS: 1. c, 2. b, 3. a, 4. b, 5. b, 6. a, 7. c, 8. a, 9. c

GLOSSARY

Affirmation
A statement that something is true. A positive affirmation is a positive statement used to challenge negative thoughts and boost self-esteem.

Augur
In ancient Rome, an augur was a priest who interpreted the will of the gods. They did this by reading signs, mainly from birds.

Babylonia
An ancient region located in southern Mesopotamia, centred around the city of Babylon.

Celestial
Relating to the sky or heaven. The Sun, Moon, stars and planets are all examples of celestial bodies.

Clairvoyant
A person who claims to be able to see things that other people cannot see. They are said to have a 'sixth sense' that goes beyond the basic five senses of hearing, sight, smell, taste and touch.

Deity
A god or supernatural being that has power over some aspect of the Universe or life and is worshipped by people.

Determinism
The idea that all events in the Universe are inevitable: everything that happens could not have happened any other way.

Divination
The practice of discovering future events or hidden knowledge by supernatural powers.

Diviner
A person who practices divination.

Fortune
Chance or luck. In the context of fortune telling, it refers to future events.

Fortune teller
A person with the supposed ability to predict the future. Fortune tellers use different methods to read a person's future.

Free will
The idea that humans have the ability to make their own decisions and choose their own path.

Horoscope
An astrological chart showing the positions of the Sun, Moon and planets at a specific moment in time. It is used for divination.

Insight
The ability to gain a deep understanding of something.

Introspection
The examination of your own thoughts and feelings.

Intuition
The ability to know something without any proof. It is often referred to as a 'gut feeling'.

Medium
A means through which something is communicated. Also, a person who has the ability to communicate with spirits.

Mesopotamia
An ancient region of southwest Asia. It is known as the birthplace of civilisation.

Mindset
A set of beliefs that influence how you think and respond to situations.

Mystic
A person who seeks to uncover divine or sacred truths through spiritual practices.

Philosopher
A person who studies or writes about the nature of knowledge, reality and existence.

Precognitive
Knowledge of a future event through mysterious ways.

Prophecy
A prediction of the future, especially one revealed by a supernatural entity, such as a deity.

Prophet
A person who is thought to be in contact with a divine being, such as God, and speaks on behalf of that being.

Psychic
A person who claims to have special mental abilities, such as the ability to tell the future.

Seer
A person who claims to be able to see into the future. Often used interchangeably with the terms 'soothsayer' and 'prophet'.

Spirituality
A practice concerned with the human spirit (the essence of a person) as opposed to physical things. Spiritual people may be religious or not.

Subconscious
The part of your mind that can influence your behaviour, even though you are not aware of it. It stores things such as memories and emotions.

Supernatural
Something that cannot be explained by science or the laws of nature.

Witchcraft
The practice of magic, especially to cause harm. Witchcraft is not the same as fortune telling.

Zodiac
An area of the sky through which the Sun, Moon and planets move. It is divided into twelve astrological signs or constellations.

INDEX

A
aeromancy 8, **54–57**
Apollo 13
Aristotle 10, 45
Artemidorus 21
Asclepius 21
astrology 8, **40–47**, 58

B
Babylon 24, 40
Babylonia 18, 19, 40, 44, 45, 54
bibliomancy 8, **64–67**
Buddhism 62

C
capnomancy 8
cartomancy 9, **30–37**
Cayce, Edgar 49
Chi Chi Sticks 63
cleromancy 9
Colman Smith, Pamela 30
communication 11, 13, 26, 35, 41, 42
crystal ball 15

D
determinism 29

E
Egypt, ancient 14, 18, 19, 20, 24
elements, the 12
Europe 14, 34, 50

F
Fortuna 19
fortune tellers 16, **48–49**, 59
France 30
free will 28, 29, 38

G
Geomancy 9
gods, the 19, 20, 55, 56
Greece, ancient 10, 14, 20, 21, 40, 54, 64

H
health 10, 11
horoscope 9, **40–43**
hydromancy 15

I
I Ching 18
India, ancient 10
Italy 30, 56

J
Jiaobei 63
Jupiter 13

K
Kau Cim 9, **60–63**

L
Lenormand, Marie Anne 35, 49
Les Prophéties (The Prophecies) 17
life path 25, 26, 27
luck 19, 24, 33, 56, 57, 62
Luna 13
Luna (goddess) 45

M
Major Arcana 31, **32–33**
Mars 13
master numbers 25, 27
Mercury 13
Mesopotamia, ancient 20, 40, 44, 45
mindset 29, 39

Minor Arcana 31, 32
Moon sign 41
Moon, the 40, 41, **44–47**
mythology, Greek 20, 56

N
new beginnings 23, 26, 32, 33, 35, 36, 45, 46
Nostradamus 15, 17, 48
numerology 9, **24–27**

O
onamancy 9
Oneirocritica 21
Oneiroi 20
oneiromancy 9, 19, **20–23**

P
palmistry 9, **10–13**
Persia, ancient 19
personality 10, 13, 25, 40, 46
precognitive dream 21
prediction 17, 28, 48, 49
psychology 29
psychometry 9
Pythagoras 24

R
relationships 35, 36, 37, 53
rising sign 41
Rome, ancient 19, 64

S
Saturn 13
science 29, 58
scrying 9, **14–17**, 19, 48
scyphomancy 19

Selene 45
stars 19, 40, 56
star sign 41, **42–43**
subconscious 16, 41
sun sign 41
Sun, the 40, 41, 45

T
Taoism 62
tarot 28, **30–33**, 35, 37
tasseography 9, **50–53**
traits 10, 12, 13, 40, 42, 43

U
Universe, the 24, 27, 45, 58, 62

V
Vanga, Baba 49
Venus 131
vibrational energy 24, 25

W
Wong, Tai Sin 62
Wong Tai Sin Temple 62

Z
zoomancy 59
zodiac 41

72